Space Begins
in the Mind

An
Introduction
to the Quantum
of
Symmetry

Buntu Nkuhlu

authorHOUSE®

AuthorHouse™ UK
1663 Liberty Drive
Bloomington, IN 47403 USA
www.authorhouse.co.uk
Phone: 0800.197.4150

Published by AuthorHouse 05/09/2018

ISBN: 978-1-5246-7763-3 (sc)
ISBN: 978-1-5246-7762-6 (e)

"Throughout the centuries there were men who took first steps down new roads armed with nothing but their own vision"-Ayn Rand

Table of Contents

Acknowledgements

This body of work is a collaborative effort by all the contributors involved.

A special thanks to AuthorHouse UK.

Acknowledgement to my father, Adv. Mxoleli Nkuhlu for affording me the space and time to concentrate on this body of work and getting it to a point of its completion. I thank my mom, Ntombentsha Beauty Nkuhlu, for her persistent encouragement and unfaltering love. Mama, I appreciate those lengthy late night conversations in your kitchen discussing The Quantum of Symmetry. I love you Mama. To my two beautiful sisters Lashie and Anathi, thank you for embracing me. Your inspirational contributions in both my life and this book are well-appreciated. I love you.

I would like to thank my friends Lwandolwethu Qasha and Oganne Shuping, for the idea of this book would not have been borne in mind were it not for them. Thanks to Koketso Mangaba, Londiwe Zwane and Keitumetse Gama, a few of my good friends who assisted me in editing and refining *An Introduction to The Quantum of Symmetry* to what it has since become.

Who would I be without uTata omkhulu Wiseman Thembekile and uMakhulu Lulama Maria Nkuhlu. I thank you for everything you have done for me. You always have and will forever be my pillars of strength, wisdom and perseverance.

I am the proud son to Ootata abasixhenxe: Mveleli, Mxoleli, Mfundo, Mandisi, Ayanda, Andile and Sabelo. I have as many mothers as I do fathers. I have learned so much just by you always being there. My belief is that, this body of work is a manifestation of some of the values which have been handed down by you to me. I am forever grateful to all of you for your presence in my life.

To uMakhulu, the awesome Vuyelwa Sodladla and my beautiful aunt, Nomonde Sodladla, I express my eternal gratitude for your constant prayers.

I thank uTata omkhulu Prof. Wiseman Lumkile and uMakhulu Hazel Nondima Nkuhlu for showing me that even under the harshest of conditions, the impossible is achievable.

The Transkei, in the Eastern Cape, beneath the mountains of Mbulukhweza, Tsomo, is where the strength and determination to write this book are sourced. To all family and friends who belong there, this book is a dedication to our homeland. To Njeya, this is for you.

To the bands Bateleur and The Brother Moves On, your music kept me writing.

I can't remember a time without the support of my uncle, Lazola Sodladla together with our close friends, Sifundo and Sihlangule Msutu. You guys mean the world to me.

Thanks to Ebenhezer Musandiwa, Dumisani Sibeko, Karabo Pooe, Stephen Knotze, the MEFXG and to all my friends who, time and time again, inspire me to be my best self.

Xola, Mbuso, Nombuso, Chulumanco, Khanyisa and all my cousins, you keep me young, invigorated and on my toes. I love you all.

To my nephew and niece, Lafika and Lisavela Bongco, you have made me a proud uncle.

In memory of Wiseman Thembekile, Lulama Maria, Mveleli, Andile and Tony Nkuhlu.

To God, my creator, thank you.

Foreword

For millennia space has been the one true medium of dominion over territory and livelihood. Space has seen Man suffer and prosper in trying to protect or occupy it. The conquering of space has yielded in abundant natural reserves. The world over space is what kingdoms were made of, what kings and queens were revered for, how mothers and fathers could ensure the continued existence of their offspring and dynasty. But, why space?

Perhaps, to answer this question we ought to first find out as to what space truly is. What does space mean to you? Is space the absence of physical matter? Does it represent land or freedom? Is it purely the fabric of the heavens? Or is space simply the air you see around you? The truth is space is all these things and more.

The Universe as we know it is said to be a consequence of about 14 billion years across space and time. Paradoxically, it is said also that the entirety of the space that makes up the Universe is the embodiment of eternity and infinity.

This paradox seems to disappear when one considers the Universe as a place where it simply cannot exist in isolation. One must reimagine a Universe of Multiverses, in other words, multiple Universes.

When it comes to uncovering the secrets of the Cosmos, it is clear that scientists are facing challenging and exciting times ahead. There is a lot that scientists still do not yet understand about the Universe, nevertheless they are making progress in leaps and bounds. Scientists have begun considering exotic and enigmatic forces such as Black Holes, Dark Matter, Dark Energy, Inflation and Quantum Entanglement.

Composed of a stream of particles the Universe and indeed the fabric of space is not at all what it seems. With the naked eye, the furthest that Man can see across space and time in real-time happens to be as far as the most advanced technology can observe. With the naked eye we can see stars that are millions of light years away.

The Universe's past, present and future are all captured within its spatial confines. For the reason that the Universe is its own quantum (measurement) one may well assume that beyond the spatial confines of the universe 'nothing' exists. All entities within the spatial confines of the Universe, ranging from the most fundamental entity to the most superfluous, are exemplified by way of the silhouette of the fabric of space. In this book, space and consequently all of matter, are an expression of the paradigms of *unity, symmetry and polarity*.

In 1687 the scientist Sir Isaac Newton published his paper *Principia Mathematica*. This paper comprised of three laws of motion. Of these laws, the most ground-breaking was the third. In his third law, Sir Isaac Newton pronounced that every action has an equal and opposite reaction. Perhaps, we are yet to fully appreciate what Newton truly meant by this. As for *The Introduction to The Quantum of Symmetry* therein lays Newton's statement the basis of all life as we know it. But before we examine and deduce Newton's observations, we ought to first make a few concessions that will support our determinations going forward.

To start with, the entire Universe in its whole is one single entity (unity). Furthermore, all constructive (and destructive) energies of the Universe between two or more entities in the Universe are dependent on two equal forces (symmetry). And finally, all constructive (and destructive) energies of the Universe between any two or more entities are dependent on two opposite forces (polarity).

With the above mentioned in mind, let us now examine and attempt to deduce Sir Isaac Newton's suggestion:

"Every action has an equal and opposite reaction"

What came first, the chicken or the egg? Is it practically possible for a snake to swallow itself whole? Does one push up against a wall or does the wall push up against them? In an attempt to answer questions of this nature what we often find is that the paradox lies not in the ability or inability to reach a valid answer, but rather in the limitations of the question itself. And just as these paradoxes beg the need to be adequately queried and responded to, so does Newton's simple but sophisticated statement, "Every action has an equal and opposite reaction".

Further down is an illustrative look at the various paradigms of Newton's suggestion, with each variation expressed through one of the three paradigms of The Quantum of Symmetry (QOS), i.e. *unity, symmetry and polarity*.

- Action and reaction are equal in force.

action   **reaction**

- Action and reaction are opposite in force.

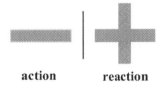

action   **reaction**

- The relationship between action and reaction is that of a symbiotic nature as one cannot exist without the other.

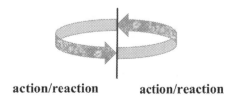

action/reaction   **action/reaction**

- The relationship between action and reaction is not as a result of the one or the other, as they may have together appeared at the same time from the initial point of existence.

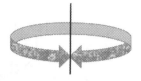

action/reaction   **action/reaction**

- As the initial point of existence is unknown, we can only assume that both action and reaction are a consequence or the product of a greater force, namely The Quantum of Symmetry.

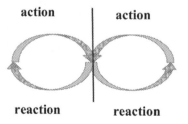

action   **action**

reaction   **reaction**

In the end what we find is that just like two sides of the same coin, Newton's 'action and reaction' cannot escape the paradigms of *unity, symmetry and polarity*. Consequently, these paradigms are the three fundamental considerations of the QOS.

The space all entities occupy in the Universe and on Earth is relatively *unified, symmetrical* and *polarised*.

Every inch of the fabric of space the Universe has ever stretched and every step Man has ever taken has been taken in consideration of this. Owing to this veracity of existence, since his inception Mankind has had to adapt in order to have optimal negotiation over his Universe's tumultuous terrain.

Through innovation in science and technology, Man has made means to break laws of physics previously believed to be un-breakable. It is not that Man can in truth break laws of physics, rather it is just that Man has yet to fully understand physics. We have made means to travel by land, sea and air safely and comfortably. However, every scientist knows that Man's glory hangs in harnessing the fundamental forces of his Universe. Passion fuels persistence in a scientist, of which can propel him or her to greatness. Every scientist's dream is to be mentioned in the same breath as Newton, Einstein, Schrödinger, Rutherford, and so forth. But what these men had in common is not just the scientific knowledge of space, time and matter. What these men had is what sets them apart from the rest, and is what cannot be taught at any institution- and that is imagination.

In *An Introduction to The Quantum of Symmetry*, when we speak of *unity, symmetry and polarity* we speak of fundamental paradigms that confine space. Contained by space are the forces of *light, time, purpose, transformation* and *uncertainty*. In an effort to make sense of the entirety of space, juxtaposed with all that which exists in it, the QOS attempts to find complementary attributes of space, ranging from the smallest to the biggest known entities to Man; the sub-atomic world to the greater Universe.

When asked by someone as to what in fact is the QOS, I almost every time find myself at a loss for words. This is because the very moment at making an attempt to explain the QOS, it soon becomes apparent that its premise is as old as time and that it is embedded in each and every part of our existence. Perhaps the simplest but nevertheless evasive way in answering this question, is that "everything has an origin, and the origin of everything is symmetry". However, this answer is like adding fuel to fire and from here on out what began as an average inquest, takes on another form, understandably.

An Introduction to The Quantum of Symmetry serves as a first edition to what is an eternal quest for knowledge and wisdom. Our ultimate destination is untainted enlightenment, if such a place exists. Hopefully, for the time being, this book will answer some of the questions I have been unable to shed light on.

More than anything, developing this book has helped me to better define the QOS. At its inception, the QOS was just but a shapeless idea, and a chaotic one at that. But then, the more I pondered on it, the more it unfurled. Before I knew it, I had put together a tangible foundation from which to form what would later be its composition.

This book was essentially written with the youth of all nations in mind, but as it progressed, there was hardly any reason why it couldn't be for everyone. Needless to say, a large portion of it is dedicated to the future and what it has in-store for us as individuals, societies and generations.

The name, 'The Quantum of Symmetry' is simply a way in which I have chosen to best articulate this idea.

I believe it is important to state that in writing, this book I have tried my best to omit the painful history in which Mankind has discriminated against each other, enslaved, oppressed, deprived and slayed one another, as this would have been an entirely different book.

In order to write this book, I have had to use two concepts of reason. Throughout this book you will find that I have referred to certain facts of the Universe and the world by using two concepts known as *Epistemology* and *Genus and Differentia*. The use of these two concepts was necessary as all the abstracts and concretes of our reality, as we know it, are founded on concepts, from time to words, all the way through to the heavens.

"*Conscious as a state of awareness, is not a passive state but an active process that consists of two essentials: differentiation and integration*"-Ayn Rand

What is *Epistemology* and *Genus and Differentia*?

<u>*Epistemology*</u> ipistemaleje

noun

The theory of knowledge, especially with regard to its methods, validity, and scope. Epistemology is the investigation of what distinguishes justified belief from opinion.

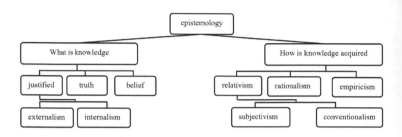

As defined and illustrated above, *Epistemology* is the quest to discover what knowledge essentially is; how it is acquired; and to what extent is it possible for a given subject or entity to be known.

<u>genus</u> jenes

noun (pl. Genera or genuses)

(in philosophical terms and general use) a class of things that have common characteristics and that can be divided into subordinate kinds.

<u>differentia</u>

noun

(chiefly philosophy) an attribute that distinguishes a species of thing from other species of the same genus.

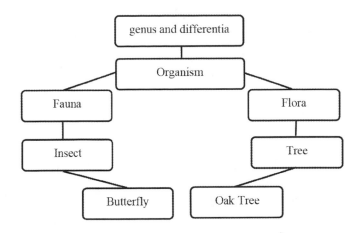

With consideration of the definition of the words 'genus' and 'differentia', above is provided an illustrative example showing how the concept functions when *Genus and Differentia* are combined. In the above illustration, the differentia is 'butterfly' and 'oak tree'. The genus is 'organism'.

Bring the concepts of *Epistemology* and *Genus and Differentia* together, and what you will have is a hierarchical way of determining the origin of any concept, and with it, its derivative.

Envisage the acquisition and succinct understanding of the implications of the concepts of *Epistemology* and *Genus and Differentia*. Whatever one is likely to come across throughout his or her life, regardless of its complexity, could be logically reduced to its most diminutive value, making any concept simpler to understand.

Alas, the mechanisms of *Epistemology* and *Genus and Differentia* are no secret, yet we seem not to appreciate the conceptual value these two concepts hold, even though we reflexively apply these two concepts each and every day of our lives. Needless to say, there is a strong feeling which drives me to arrive to the conclusion that the knowledge and application of *Epistemology* and *Genus and Differentia* should be emphasised within the realms of institutional education, particularly for scholars in their earliest definitive years. Combined, these two concepts should be incorporated as a life-orientated program for purposes of an all-embracing approach towards literacy, numeracy and beyond. I believe that the earlier in life the combination of *Epistemology* and *Genus and Differentia* is taught concisely and comprehensively, The sooner one can improve the capacity to optimally understand oneself against his world.

So, what is The Quantum of Symmetry (QOS)?

I could say that the QOS is a philosophical memoir. I could say that it is a scientific hypothesis. I could very well say that the QOS is a conceptual representation of a fundamental force. However, the QOS always proves to be more than just what it seems to be.

The QOS is the measurement of the paradigms and forces of space. The QOS on the most fundamentally conceivable human level, is the practice and the finesse that assists one to thoughtfully navigate one's consciousness and intuition. It is a tool which arms one with a more attuned and relevant subconscious in harmony with one's Universe.

For argument's sake, imagine yourself in an uneasy environment. Wouldn't it be vital for you to have nothing short of an untouched experience of outlook and self-introspection in accordance to what could indeed be happening around you? Without this consideration, wouldn't you be more susceptible to easily making the grievous mistake of imparting a negative reaction to what in fact has not (yet) even taken place?

The QOS as a conceptual instrument is not corporeal. It is an abstract of the mind. In other words, if the brain were the hardware of a supercomputer, the mind would be its software and the QOS would be the supercomputer's coding platform.

Visualize the bearer of the QOS as an energy reactor, and in this energy reactor mechanisms to not only better take in and discharge energy concurrently, but also to better manipulate it. The bearer of the QOS would have to neutralize energy only to accentuate it. the QOS would therefore make for the necessary calibration of the balancing act between positive and negative, good and evil, light and darkness, life and death, and everything in between.

At its optimum, the QOS should act as an ever-active measurement or gauge of the balance of energies. Imagine the QOS as a simultaneous and infinite back-and-forth surge of polarization between two points, always convening at the centre. Going forward, it will be imperative that the reader understands that the struggle of all variations of energy are not between negative and positive, but the struggle is between the centre and its extremes.

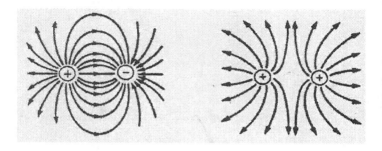

The interaction between the centre and its extremes

Note that *unity, symmetry and polarity* are at the heart of this book and it is advisable that even whilst reading it, you keep this in mind, with the purpose of not deviating from its theme. By the reader assuming an either negative or positive stance on the contents of this book whilst not having fully understood its implications, he or she will have pre-maturely defeated its purpose and therefore the book itself will prove futile. Once the reader has read through the book and fully understood its crux, naturally, the manner in which to apply the QOS, or whether or not to apply it at all, is entirely up to the reader, not that one really has a choice.

Now that we've gotten that out of the way, let's get right down to it.

Symmetry

A human being's anatomical proportion is evidence of the existence of symmetry. The symmetry in us is a remnant of our past. It is mind-boggling to think that through the entire Universe's turbulent history, Mankind would be formed. Looking back, the materials that would later create Mankind have always been there. This means that our existence had long been awaited.

But how did this come to be?

In 1850, a scientist by the name William Rankine, first used the term *Law of the Conservation of Energy*. This term best described a revolutionary idea that would define the face of science as we know it. As per the empirical *Law of the Conservation of Energy,* the energy in the Universe cannot be created or destroyed, neither does it increase or decrease. Rather, the energy in the Universe is transformed from one form to another. The *Law of the Conservation of Energy* postulates that from its initial point of conception, up to today, the amount of energy in the Universe and indeed the energy that formed the Earth and everything in it, has remained conserved; but has since been dispersed as a result of the expansion of the fabric of space.

To elucidate the trueness of the expansion of the fabric of space, we have celestial bodies as proof. A star that is a million light-years away looks today as it did a million years ago. This means that when we look up to the sky and gaze at a star, we are in fact looking back into millions of years ago. In order to understand the expansion of the fabric of space, we have to appreciate the nature of light.

A light-year is a measure of great distances. Light travels at almost 300 000 km per second in a vacuum. According to these numbers, in a year, light will have travelled a distance of approximately 9,5 trillion km (one light-year). Hypothetically, if the light of a star that is a million light years away were to go off and then on again, light would have to travel approximately 9,5 trillion km or one light-year, multiplied by a million to reach planet Earth again. Between two points, in this case the first being as far as the naked eye can see, and the second, a star that is a million light-years away, it is revealed to us how a star, and in fact, the Universe would have looked a million years ago. Because time is determined by space, it means that the celestial bodies we see in real-time have been in existence for a very long time but are, as a consequence of the expansion of space, farther. With the naked eye, we can see stars that are millions of light years away, however, we can not tell their exact distances. That is why when we look at the stars, it becomes impossible to tell which ones are closer or farther. With advanced stellar viewing apparatus, scientists have now found various ways to detect how near or how far stars are from planet Earth.

To get a sense of these numbers, a year has in it 525600 minutes. It takes light 525600 minutes to travel about 9,5 trillion km. Our sun is approximately 150 million km away from planet Earth. It takes the light of the sun roughly 8 minutes to reach planet Earth.

All of that which every inhabitant of the Cosmos perceives, relies on the forces of *light, time, purpose, transformation* and *uncertainty,* all being within the confines of space. In other words, every inch of space of the Universe, at any given moment or event in time, is governable by these five forces. The forces of *light, time, purpose, transformation* and *uncertainty* within the confines of space, are contained in the earlier mentioned paradigms of the QOS: *unity, symmetry and polarity.*

Below is a simple illustration representing how a conceptualist of the QOS should invariably perceive his or her Universe.

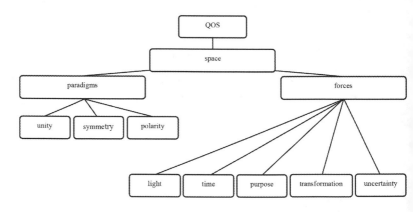

How a conceptualist sees reality, relies entirely on how he perceives it and what sensations he experiences whilst perceiving it. The only impediment that could hinder a conceptualist's way of thought is his frame of mind. This balancing act between the conceptualist's mind and reality takes place at different levels of complexity. The judgement of the space a conceptualist engages could either be detrimental or beneficial to the conceptualist. When a conceptualist engages space using the QOS, *time, light, transformation, purpose* and *uncertainty* are the fundamental forces of his reality. Nevertheless, no matter how infallible a concept may be, the mind can be influenced. However, were a conceptualist practice to optimally reign over his mind, so much so that, at every given moment or event in time, the three paradigms (*unity, symmetry, and polarity*) of the QOS are as the conceptualist perceives them, attuned to these five forces, he could ultimately influence the manner of things in and around his space.

We tend to say that we live in a three or a four dimensional Universe. However, even though it may seem that all works in three's (or four's), there is one aspect that we tend to overlook. This one thing is the beauty of the conceptualist's vantage point, for the reason that, to a conceptualist, an entity in existence is in existence merely by his senses, and were it not for his senses, then the conceptualist would naturally not have the knowledge of what the entity was, if it were anything at all. This purports that, in any given situation, a conceptualist of the QOS can at any given moment or event in time, take the conscious decision to be just but an observer and remove himself from whatever it is that is happening around him, although, he is very much a part of it. This means that, in a three or four dimensional world, a conceptualist of the QOS operates in the third, fourth, fifth and beyond.

A conceptualist of the QOS is something short of an alchemist. Sure, most know that all matter has an atomic basis. However, the question always remains as to what exactly is inside the atom's nucleus; and that thereof (from the atom's absolute centre to its definite exterior)? This is a question fit for a conceptualist.

Contrary to popular belief, the smallest thing known to Man is neither the atom nor its nucleus, but is a plethora of elementary particles such as quarks, leptons, bosons and electrons in a sub-atomic world full of infinite possibilities. The various combinations of these sub-atomic particles make up the many different types of atoms and are the building blocks of physical reality as we see it. These minute particles are known as quanta, plural for quantum. These quanta are entrenched in every aspect of our lives, from the air we breathe to the water we drink. This is the revolutionary world of a branch of science known as Quantum Mechanics and here, classical sciences do not apply.

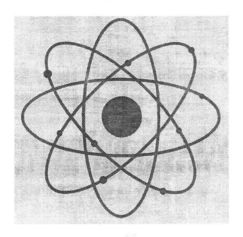

The Atom

As we set out on a quest to attribute the life of quanta to that of ours, we ought to find a complementary characteristic which might substantiate our mutual existence...

Quantum Mechanics suggests that the Universe began in a state of unity and complete symmetry. In the twinkle of an eye preceding the Big Bang, the entire Universe would have just been the size of the tip of a ball-point pen. In just that one speck, there must have been all of the Universe's energy. Unity would constitute symmetry, which would in turn comprise polarity. Although little is known of this moment, what we do know we have defined.

This brings us to what the world has come to know as Planck's constant (*h*). Named after the physicist Max Planck, Planck's constant is an arithmetic unit which expresses the value of all quanta. Planck's constant has to be the most fundamental unit of measurement.

Discovered by Peter Higgs, the most fundamental of all quanta is the Higg's boson, otherwise known as the 'God particle'. As Quantum Mechanics would have it, the Higg's boson is believed to be the first known entity to have ever existed. The 'God particle' is said to be the quantum that gives mass to all other particles. This force particle is said to be the embodiment of perfect unity and absolute symmetry. At the right time and in the ideal conditions, the first ever Higg's boson would rupture and later bring into existence a polarised pair of photons and with it, the expansion of the fabric of space and time, which would ultimately come to be known as the Big Bang.

The pair of photons were equal in terms of force but were polarised in terms of matter in the sense that, they each spun in two different directions, either clockwise or anti-clockwise, only to convene at the centre. The merge between these two photons is what physicists call Constructive Interference, as the meeting of a pair of photons spews out the fabric of space and time and subsequently constructs *matter* and *force fields*. But unlike the perfectly symmetrical Higg's boson, each half of the pair of photons and subsequently all *matter* would be asymmetrical and polarised. However, reminiscent of the perfectly symmetrical Higg's boson, the *force fields* of each half of the pair of photons and subsequently all matter, would maintain their symmetry. This is how the beginning of the known Universe was set in motion.

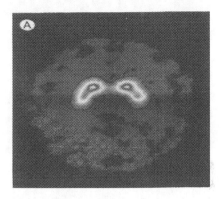

A pair of photons equal in force spinning in two opposite directions.

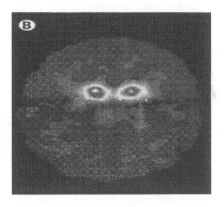

The pair of photons convening at the centre, about to merge.

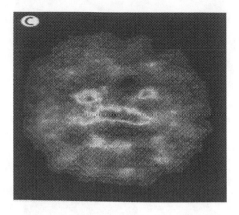

The pair of photons merged. Constructive interference spewing out the fabric of space-time and constructing matter and force-fields.

Constructive interference would thereafter put into motion a series of events, which would facilitate the establishment of an environment in which organisms would later exist, adapt and reproduce. By observing the Universe, great minds would soon realise that on closer inspection, the Cosmos followed a rule of hierarchy. Matter is composed of quanta; quanta make up atoms; atoms make up molecules; and molecules make up cells. All are governed by *unity, symmetry and polarity* and in turn, all are governable by *time, light, transformation, purpose* and *uncertainty*.

Human beings themselves are subject to symmetry. Contrary to popular belief symmetry in us goes way beyond a superficial trait. In humans, symmetry exhibits not only proportion but also health, beauty and functionality. One need not ponder too hard on how fundamental the feature of the combination of *symmetry, unity* and *polarity* is as an aspect of both courtship and reproduction in the nature of organisms.

While on the subject of courtship and reproduction, let us touch on how the conception of a human being takes place. The average human being has 46 chromosomes, of which are composed in 2 pairs of 23. Each half of the pair is inherited from both parents. Chromosomes carry genes and genes are composed of DNA. All of this takes place pending the fusion of a female's egg cell and a male's sperm cell, resulting in a fertilized egg.

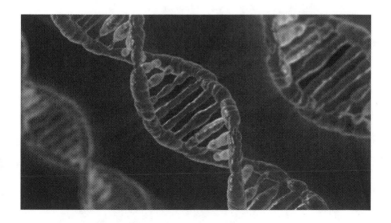

The DNA Helix

A human foetus starts off as one cell. The one cell then splits perfectly in the middle to form two cells. The two cells then split into four cells, and so on. In the end, the fully formed foetus has half of each parent infused in its genome. This process is called cell division and bears all the signs of the three paradigms of QOS, i.e. *unity, symmetry and polarity*. Without *unity, symmetry and polarity*, cell division simply would not take place. Like the Universe, a human life starts off as a small, unified entity. In that one small organism, exists all the potential energy that the human life will ever come to need in order for it to become a fully formed foetus.

Below is an illustration of how one cell splits into two cells during cell division.

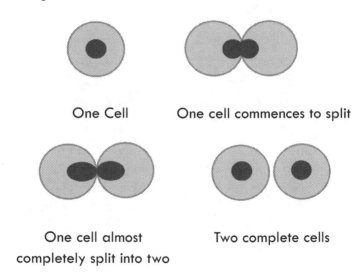

One Cell

One cell commences to split

One cell almost completely split into two

Two complete cells

Cell division is indicative of what the QOS strives to prove. Firstly, that the Universe and everything in it was, a long time ago, unified and completely symmetrical. Secondly, that the balance of energy in the Universe is epitomised through *unity, symmetry and polarity*. Additionally, that the polarity and equilibrium of negative and positive forces are necessary for our existence. And finally, that in the right place, at the right moment and under the right conditions is how creation finds its purpose, but not without submitting to change and uncertainty.

Human beings, just like atoms and cells, potentially possess the infinite power to adjust and transform the space they occupy. This feat takes dedicated and steadfast conceptualists with a somewhat removed and untouched perception of the volatile world in which we exist. The inability to recognise our potential to be better is our biggest downfall. Potential is the power to become.

With all that happens between ourselves and the Universe, the world does its part in that, it becomes a canvas for how one perceives one's reality; displaying the beautiful flaws that paint a picture of imperfection in the midst of a desire of a Utopian way of life.

With all that people see, some choose to ignore the bigger picture. Possibly because their lives are led by entities such as money and power, as these are secularly believed to be the measure of one's success. But how far can the insatiable pursuit of money and power take us? And what implications is it accompanied by, not only as individuals, but more importantly as a civilization?

The mistake conceptualists often make is that, we attempt to make use of only what is already there, yet we have both the capacity and the ability to conceive and initiate bigger and better mechanisms of the world. It is frightening when one thinks of the potential we as the human race have, but ever so often, the problem some of us are faced with is that we cannot connect the pieces of 'the jigsaw puzzle'; and of those of us who can, in most instances, never find the time to put together the pieces. This is due mainly to the breakdown of the mentor-apprentice relationship between conceptualists. The world needs innovative conceptualists, but what is of most importance is that such innovators be intellectually and emotionally mature enough to become mentors within their respective craft.

Be advised, the QOS has its soft undertones and its extreme overtones, depending on how a conceptualist chooses to utilise it as a model of his or her life. As with any other ideal, the QOS can, by its bearer, be used innocently or maliciously over the people concerned.

Before readers had picked up this book, the QOS, as the author's conception, was known only to him, yet its premise is and always has been embedded in everything and in each and every one of us. This is proof that in essence, the QOS is to be first and foremost an all-inclusive concept. And so, for all intents and purposes, every reasonable person ought to possess the capacity to know what the QOS is. With that said, below is an example that attempts to put across its simplistic nature.

Imagine two entities radiating energy in a room, both of which are unfamiliar with the premise of the QOS and therefore unable to conceive it. We will say that each of them has the energy of a 50% relative to the sum total of the energy in the room of a 100%. With their 50%, they each can change the energy in the room to either good or bad. And so, the energy in the room is divided into two parts, as there are two of them. To keep the energy in the room stable, the two entities will both have to contribute a variation of positive and/or negative energy equal to the sum total of a 100%. So, what you now have are two entities of which both are unfamiliar to the premise of the QOS, each contributing a variation of positive and negative energy and collectively having to keep the energy in the room at a threshold of a 100%. This will prove to be a painstaking-shift as neither of them has clear middle-ground.

The energy of each entity relative to the room (both of which are unfamiliar to the premise of the QOS)

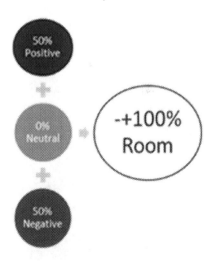

Imagine now, having made just one of the two entities in the room attuned to the premise of the QOS. The struggle ceases to be between negative and positive. The struggle for this one entity has since become between the centre and its extremes. And so, the best way for it to better express its energy, whether negative and/or positive, would be to neutralise the energy in the room, only to accentuate it. This way, regardless of what energy its counterpart may exude, whether negative or positive, the overriding energy will always be controlled by the bearer of the QOS.

The energy of the bearer of the QOS is relative to his counterpart's energy and the sum of energy in the room

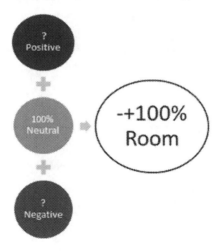

The QOS is a finesse to its bearer. The bearer of the QOS has to, after and/ or during each discreet significant event, directly or indirectly rein in whatever conflict he is faced with. He does this by firstly quantifying the symmetry against its extremes, proceeding on to neutralise the energy and after, has to accentuate the resultant energy such that it, becomes the desired energy.

Space, Time, Light

According to the QOS, given the limitless reaches of space, every split-second is an opportunity for a spontaneous event to transpire. If Man is to make any significant efforts in trying his hand at taming the Universe, he must realise that time as he knows it, does not exist, as time to him is just a tool of measurement between two or more points in space. Space is energy and energy is space. So, at all times, and for as long as he is conscious of it, space is the most valuable asset available to him.

The story of space is one that goes back a long way; before the Mass-dominated era; before the Grand Unification, and even before the birth of time itself. To better understand the profundity of space, it is essential that one appreciates the empirical implications of the Space-Time relationship.

Like Earth's continents, galaxies in the past were much closer together. This evocative past would later come to be known as the era of Grand Unification. And if the postulation of the theory of the Grand Unification is plausible, it would mean that, at one time in the life of the Universe, everything existed as one, just as galaxies and the Earth's continents; and in essence, that the Universe was in itself symmetrical. Because all the space in the Universe was so congested, particles led lives of no significance and died instantaneously as there was neither time nor space to exist in.

In a nutshell, through the spontaneous interaction of fundamental particles, space would be spawned, and therefore time would exist with galaxies moving further away from each other, making space less dense and less congested.

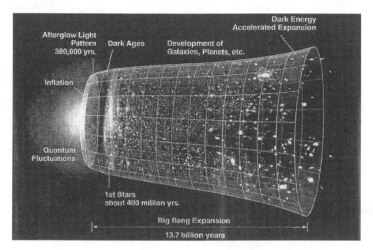

The expansion of the Big Bang

Questions arise as to what brought on the Mass-dominated era post the era of Grand Unification? What caused this complete symmetry to break? What caused galaxies, suns, planets and moons to form? What caused the end of the era of Grand Unification?

What the hypothesis of the Mass-dominated era suggests is simple. The bigger the mass of an entity, the more gravitational force it has and the more entities with less mass, are likely to orbit it, just as the planets orbit the Sun and the moons orbit the planets.

The Solar System

The ultimate question becomes, how did organisms come about? And what does Man, in fact, have to do with the Grand Unification and the Mass-dominated eras? It is a straight-forward question worthy of a straight-forward answer, right? Not entirely. To find answers to the past, there is a need to query the present.

Photosynthesis has to be one of Nature's most impressive creations. Photosynthesis is a big deal, as it lays down the groundwork of how the coming together of water and light is the cause of the creation of all biological life on Earth as we know it.

And so, the story goes. Tucked away in the corner of the Universe, in some far-away galaxy, in the waters of a planet called Earth-was the place. *Precambrian* was the time. The Sun was the light and creation was the purpose. The effervescence for life was brewing by way of photosynthesis and we were to be its produce. Mother Nature would dictate that packets of light from the Sun radiate through every single prismatic drop of the waters, inducing a multitude of colours.

Mother Nature would then proceed to conjure up bacteria, from which coral would yield. Under her command, fish would swim, serpents would slither, birds would fly, flowers would bloom and Man would walk.

But one cannot talk about photosynthesis without mentioning light and one can't talk about light without mentioning Man's most resourceful information rendering organ-the eye.

We exist as a matter of light which, when combined with water, brings into being organisms. Without taking anything away from the other sense organs, the eye just so happens to be the most ideal organ to witness and exemplify Mother Nature's marvels.

Within the context of the QOS, photosynthesis, light and the eye, all have one common inherent force known as electromagnetism.

As rays of light enter the eye, it transforms and transmits these rays to the brain in the form of electrical signals. When these electrical signals reach the brain, only then are they definable as images because, all by itself, all that the eye can conceive is light and not the image itself.

Eyes are an evolutionary circumstance and only start to show up in our planet's earliest, most fundamental life forms as eye spots. It is said that the Earth is $4\frac{1}{2}$ billion years old and that bacteria lived as long ago as $3\frac{1}{2}$ billion years. One thousand, one hundred million years ago, invertebrates such as flatworms and starfish, with light-sensitive areas on their bodies in the form of eye spots, emerged. These elementary life forms could distinguish only between light and dark. This distinction allowed these simple organisms to measure how near or far they ought to be from the surface of the oceans. Intended for nutritional purposes, all this was done by sensing how much light penetrated the water, as too little or too much would mean almost certain demise.

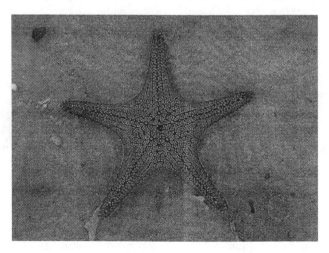

The Starfish

The Flatworm

Fast-forward to about 2 million years ago. The epoch of Man begins and so have his eyes evolved. Man has stereoscopic vision, which means he can perceive the thickness of objects and can judge depth and distance. But this would not be as possible were it not for his binocular vision (synchronization of both eyes).

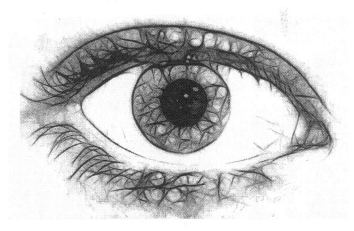

The Human Eye

His eye is clearly more superior to that of the flatworm and starfish and more complex. In the retina of his eye are light-sensitive cells called rods and cones. Rods enable him to see shades of grey and cones absorb rays of red, green and blue. His eye has become so advanced that the variations of these three pigments allow him to distinguish more than 200 colours. Depth perception through length, breadth and height enables him to perceive his 3 dimensional world.

The rays red, green and blue are each quite special in their uniqueness. We enjoy the privileges that come with vision as a cause of these three rays. However, get a glimpse of the earlier mentioned force called electromagnetism and you will realise that there is more to light than meets the eye.

All the light conceivable to a human being's naked eye is known as visible light. Visible light is one of seven scientifically recognised kinds of electromagnetic waves in what is called the electromagnetic spectrum. The wavelength of various waves ranges from shortest to longest and from highest to lowest. The shorter the wave, the higher the frequency. The longer the wave, the lower the frequency. The higher the frequency, the shorter the reach of the wave. In other words, the frequency of each wave is inversely proportional to its wavelength.

The energy in the wavelength of an electromagnetic wave is determined by the vibration of the rate of electrons traversing in between each and every existent energy source. The slower the vibration of the rate of electrons, the longer the wavelength of the electromagnetic wave. The easiest of all wavelengths to produce are long waves, otherwise known as radio waves.

As with any other fundamental particle, the Universe could not possibly exist without the interaction of electrons. The electron is a fundamental sub-atomic unit of matter worth mentioning because what is an atom without an electron? What is anything for that matter?

Electrons are the lightest particles that have electrical charge. Therefore, in order for there to be an interaction between any two atomic particles, there has to be a sub-atomic electron interaction between the two atoms.

The electron is what makes the 'real world' work. It is what gives the periodic table of elements its logic. As per the periodic table of elements, the number of electrons orbiting an element's nucleus is equal to the atomic number of the element. Hydrogen is the first element in the periodic table of elements. Hydrogen's atomic number is 1. Its nucleus is orbited by one electron. Carbon is the sixth element in the periodic table of elements and its atomic number is 6. Carbon's nucleus is orbited by 6 electrons. The list of elements goes on and on. All and all, there are well over 100 known elements in the periodic table.

PERIODIC TABLE OF THE ELEMENTS

1 H																	2 He
3 Li	4 Be											5 B	6 C	7 N	8 O	9 F	10 Ne
11 Na	12 Mg											13 Al	14 Si	15 P	16 S	17 Cl	18 Ar
19 K	20 Ca	21 Sc	22 Ti	23 V	24 Cr	25 Mn	26 Fe	27 Co	28 Ni	29 Cu	30 Zn	31 Ga	32 Ge	33 As	34 Se	35 Br	36 Kr
37 Rb	38 Sr	39 Y	40 Zr	41 Nb	42 Mo	43 Tc	44 Ru	45 Rh	46 Pd	47 Ag	48 Cd	49 In	50 Sn	51 Sb	52 Te	53 I	54 Xe
55 Cs	56 Ba	57 La	72 Hf	73 Ta	74 W	75 Re	76 Os	77 Ir	78 Pt	79 Au	80 Hg	81 Tl	82 Pb	83 Bi	84 Po	85 At	86 Rn
87 Fr	88 Ra	89 Ac	104 Rf	105 Db	106 Sg	107 Bh	108 Hs	109 Mt	110 Ds	111 Rg	112 Cn	113 Uut	114 Uuq	115 Uup	116 Uuh	117 Uus	118 Uuo

58 Ce	59 Pr	60 Nd	61 Pm	62 Sm	63 Eu	64 Gd	65 Tb	66 Dy	67 Ho	68 Er	69 Tm	70 Yb	71 Lu
90 Th	91 Pa	92 U	93 Np	94 Pu	95 Am	96 Cm	97 Bk	98 Cf	99 Es	100 Fm	101 Md	102 No	103 Lr

The Periodic Table

Only electrically charged particles acquiesce to electromagnetism. However, particles such as the photon and the Higg's boson do not need charge to acquiesce to electromagnetism. In fact, the photon and the Higg's boson do not have charge. As two of the most fundamental and symmetrical forces in the Universe, the photon and the Higg's boson are exempt from charge. All known particles and forces are acquiescent to gravity. This means that, in relation to all other known forces existent in the Universe, gravity is considered to be negative energy, while all other energy is positive. But before we stray too far off, let us go back to electromagnetism.

Below is an illustration of what is called the electromagnetic spectrum.

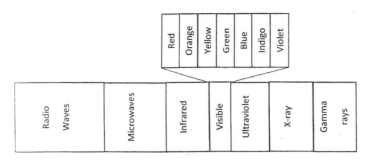

The Electromagnetic Spectrum

The seven different wavelengths or rays of the electromagnetic spectrum are gamma rays (highest in frequency and shortest in length), X-rays, ultraviolet light, visible light, infrared rays, microwaves and radio waves (lowest in frequency and longest in length), respectively.

All electromagnetic waves have the properties of light, which means that they can be reflected, diffracted, refracted and all travel at the speed of light (approximately 300, 000 kilometres per second).

Electromagnetism is one of the most fundamental forces of the Cosmos. It is a combination of electricity and magnetism. What makes the combination of these two energies so unique is how they complement each other.

Man's ability to understand electricity and magnetism, independently and collectively, is one of his greatest quests yet.

But, how does electromagnetism work? And equally important, what has it got to do with the QOS and everything we have mentioned in this chapter?

The combination of a negative and a positive force, such as that found in an electrical current, generates magnetism. This means that whenever a negative and a positive particle meet, there exists an electric field and therefore, a magnetic field. The strength of electric force is always equal to the strength of magnetic force. Be it with the nucleus and electron; atom and molecule; planet and moon; physical and metaphysical; gravity and all else; the interaction between negative and positive and thus electromagnetism, is apparent in any two or more things that have ever co-existed in the Universe.

Electromagnetism is the link to what seems to be a disparity between physics, chemistry, biology, technology, philosophy, and so on. Electromagnetism reveals to us the synergy and metaphysics between ourselves and all matter. It is a tool that assists man to measure, compare and deduce the fundamentals of the past, present and future of our Cosmos through the use of radiation.

We experience the awesome power of electromagnetism every day. We use gamma rays to treat cancer patients by unleashing the power of the radioactive element radium. X-rays are used to see through flesh, in order to treat patients with broken bones. Every day we cook with the power of hard-body radiation with infrared rays. Telecommunications companies employ microwaves to beam signals between cellular phones and other digital devices. Radio waves are used by broadcasting companies to stream sounds and images onto our radios and television sets. Visible light is how humans are able to visually distinguish between different shades of colour. Electromagnetism dominates the realms of space, time and light. It affirms the connection between ourselves and the Universe.

It just so happens that one of the most expensive machines ever built, is one dedicated to the study of the sub-atomic world of quanta. This quantum mechanics machine is housed in the most complex laboratory ever conceived by Man, called CERN or European Organisation for Nuclear Research, formerly known as Conseil Europeen pour la Recherché Nucleaire. CERN was founded in 1954.

Arguably, the most critical piece of equipment at the CERN laboratory is the most advanced particle accelerator ever built, known as the Large Hadron Collider (LHC). The particle accelerator has the capability to accelerate sub-atomic particles to high velocities, causing them to smash into each other. The LHC is situated at a mean depth of 100m underground. Spanning over 27 kilometres across France and Switzerland, near Geneva, one of the LHC'S initial goals was to find in the fleeting realm of the sub-atomic world, the enigmatic Higg's Boson, also known as the 'God Particle'. Eventually, scientists did get to have unprecedented glimpse into what they believed was the mass-giving particle. This was to be one of the most cutting-edge discoveries not only for the scientific world, but also for ordinary folk, as the discovery of the Higg's boson would surely bring in its train innovative solutions to long-standing problems.

Consciousness

Humans are entrusted with five senses consisting of seeing, feeling, taste, smell and hearing, and from the time we are born, we begin to learn how to effectively use our senses. We become conscious of space and subsequently, become more and more aware of the repercussions of not adhering to the laws of physics. Even though we have not yet developed ample logic to optimally tackle its terrain, we are undeterred by engaging and interacting with space that by the time we enter into the pre-logical phase of our lives, we have become accustomed to the fundamentals of adapting to it.

From an early age, we learn about good and bad and are encouraged to always separate the one from the other, even though these two concepts are ceaselessly inseparable. Unfortunately, the human realm of the Universe is not as simple as good from bad or positive and negative. There are disparities in the way each and every one perceives how things ought to be done. One thing is clear, positive and negative accompany each other, precisely because of the conflict and reconciliation between these two forces. Does this then not presuppose the world as a place of many contradictions?

The Chinese Yin Yang(good and evil)

It has been repeatedly proven that to resolve a conflict, one has to get to the bottom of it by simplifying it. What is equally important is that the conflict be kept amalgamated, even in its abstracted state, for it not to lose its structure or basis. In this chapter, you will see that as a concept, this is what in all its prominence the QOS aims to achieve, with special consideration to the complexities of the nature of Man's consciousness.

As the science of the mind tells us, there are three stages at which human beings process information. These stages include all that which we will ever come to know of the consciousness of Man. In the study of psychoanalytic perspective, these stages are known as the id, ego, and superego.

The first stage is the manner in which we feel, hear, smell, taste and see, in other words, sense. Sensation on its own is an untainted primary mechanism of the consciousness that humans possess in order to interact with their environment. Humans without sensation may as well be insentient because without sensation, everything we have come to know of the world ceases to exist.

The first stage is initiated by the id. The id is an intuitive component of the psychoanalytic perspective and roughly contemplates the balance of life and death/good and bad. It is a blunt and shrewd instrument of consciousness, as it operates on the basis that anything bad for the well-being of the individual is the opposite of life itself. It is completely removed from the concretes of reality and has no consideration of societal views since, by its means, society is non-existent. Propel this component to work chiefly for the benefit of the grand scheme of things and you will have achieved the optimal use of the QOS.

The second stage is the ego. The ego helps process the sensations we go through each and every second of everyday. It is one thing to feel but a completely different thing to feel and perceive what you sense. Without perception, there can be no recognition of sensation. In blunter words, it is like being pierced by a million needles and not feeling a thing at all merely because of the incapability to register the tactile sensation of pain. So, if one's perception of how he or she goes through sensations is thwarted, then the hindrance will somewhat be coherent with the end-result.

In order to propel the aforementioned id towards good, not only for the benefit of the individual but also for those around him, the ego of the psychoanalytical perspective is engaged. The ego is the mediator between what is happening inside an individual and what is happening around him. As difficult as it may be, it is vital that the ego assumes a pristine and unprejudiced role relative to the correlation between an individual's instincts and the expectations of the world.

The third and final stage at which we perceive and fully comprehend sensations as they occur, is the conceptual stage. The conceptual stage is how we base what we feel on perception (abstract) by attaching it to the reality (concrete) of the world through concepts and experiences. This is where conflict and resolution reconcile. It is a lot easier to comprehend what a thing is when comparing one thing to another; and how it became that way, particularly if it is recognisable, thus apprehending the knowledge of what its purpose is and/or what is likely to become of it. In the psychoanalytic world, this is what is known as the superego and what most of us refer to as the conscience.

The superego is the calibration of the first and second stage. It provides the individual ample control over how he chooses to perceive concretes in reality, without exempting himself from conflict and reconciliation. In the superego are contained concepts through experience, along with the knowledge gained from them. The superego as a component of the psychoanalytic perspective is the head-quarters of learning and is where the QOS as a concept dwells.

When all three stages have been assembled and processed in the correct order without any inconsistencies, it then becomes simpler to dismantle them in an attempt to individually analyse and critique them.

id	ego	superego
INSTINCTS	REALITY	MORALITY

All and all, this is what is referred to as cognition and cognition is what ideas are born out of. But, were there to be irreconcilable inconsistencies between the stages, such as those known in psychoanalysis as intrapsychic conflicts, they could cause a malfunction of the psyche, resulting in a brain associated disorder.

One sense which is seldom mentioned is the sixth sense or extrasensory perception (ESP). ESP uses an individual's pure intuition and instinct as a sensory medium. One example of extrasensory perception would be that of echolocation. Blind people are said to possess this ESP. The blind have a heightened sense of hearing. Their hearing is so advanced that they are able to tell the arrangement and displacement of objects by interpreting reflected sounds in space. Even though at most times extrasensory perception is benign, we all possess it, yet only a few have the propensity to summon it. This is, for the most part, due to everyday distractions. Our senses are susceptible to more than just the physical realm and thus need to be recognised, groomed and protected.

"The subconscious is responsible for the registering of sensation into perception, which comes about spontaneously, and is the raw automation of the cognitive mind at the bottommost point of awareness. At a higher point of awareness, is the psychological frame of mind of an individual, of which is accessible by one's own volition."- Ayn Rand

It is imperative for one to understand that all that which humans know is based on how we each use our cognitive mind to reach an idea relative to the external world. The consciousness of a living human being is an ever-active process; and that whether or not one is awake, it dares not come to a halt.

Imagine the inception of an idea as an average double-storey house you have never been in before, with multiple rooms. As you enter through the front door, you have a vantage point at which you get a feel of where it would be ideally wise to go next. Once inside, you realise that there are numerous doors which are shut and you immediately assume that through each of them, is a room and that the stairs before you lead not to just any rooms, but most probably bedrooms. Since you are on the bottom-most floor, the lounge and kitchen should be within the vicinity, right? It would be most probable.

An average double-storey house

The aforementioned is a paradigm of the capacity to construct an idea. This is done by differentiation of its components from other particular concretes, dissecting its characteristics in order to reach a more precise and in-depth conclusion by means of integration. It is just as you imagined; being at the front door only to find that through it, might be more doors leading to different rooms. It is an example of the collaboration between an individual's keen senses, his cognition and the physical world. Take into consideration that your logical cognisance is active and is simultaneously processing everything as it is being perceived. With that said, appreciate the fact that even the smallest of distractions could hinder your advancement.

The ingenuity produced by the human cognitive mind could never be simulated by any other living species on Earth. The depth at which a human being can conceive and formulate an idea is unmatched. Hence, it is essential that one appreciates the spirit of learning various fundamental concepts. The sooner an individual realises and grasps a concept, the simpler it becomes for him or her to put the world in a 'box', in an attempt to better understand it without it losing its distinctiveness, as long as the concept remains absolute wherever applicable. As a conceptual tool, the QOS does precisely that, where we find all that which we know of as the world, is governed by a law of balance and proportion, in which symmetry is the mediator of both negative and positive.

Application

What is unique about the QOS and any other succinct theoretical hypothesis for that matter, is that whether or not one learns of it, one is still, by virtue of its existence, enveloped within the lattice of the concept's framework. Surely, we would all agree that a knowledgeable individual is indeed a responsible one. Even if an individual had read this book and not applied its premise, its implications would still later than never have been unavoidable. A true concept need not be unreservedly abided by in order for it to thrive, as such a means to determine it would inevitably prove to be adversely altruistic. Rather, a true concept ought to be naturally understandable. Additionally, for all intents and purposes, it should, once an individual learns of it, be about whether or not the individual indeed understands it and what it stands for. From a purely scientific perspective, the QOS serves as an information tool, which assists in making mankind aware of his Universe. From a purely philosophical perspective, it is a text that is intended to inspire good in the individual and in all of life itself.

The QOS does not apply just to human beings and/or living organisms but applies to everything in the physical and ethereal Universe. However, because we are human beings, and boast an incredible mental capacity; a mental capacity that no other living organism can possess, our potential to connect with our Universe is unrivalled.

Naturally, most animals have an uncomplicated way of performing whatever action. Most animals either do one thing or the other. A decision taken by an animal may be as simple as a yes or a no; 1 or 0; fight or flee and beyond that, there may not be much perceptive diligence at play. On the contrary, under observation, devoid of any experimental conditions, a human being is the most unpredictable subject, simply because there is so much data that the observer would have to analyse and critique with regard to a human subject. Unlike an animal, a human being can perform complex tasks through experience, intelligence and practice by tapping into his or her conscious mind. However, the ability to do this is one that extends all the way through to a human being's capacity to reach into the subconscious mind using extrasensory projection. For instance, a 'superhuman ability' present in an individual, usually requires that the individual momentarily engages some form of extrasensory projection for the performance of the 'phenomenon' to be realised.

The QOS is not bound by limitations such as those of the five senses. It is fundamentally propelled by extrasensory projection and therefore, as a concept, has to be limitless. As its bearer, you are the measure of the QOS, thus you are the only one who can quantify your position against any other entity existent in the realm of the Universe. It would seem that the Universe has made it a point that Man be the measure of all things.

The QOS acts as an intermediary between physical and metaphysical forces. For example, a person's mind is a metaphysical manifestation of his or her brain. The mind can permeate spaces and places that would otherwise be physically impossible for the brain to grace. This too applies to a person's body and soul. It would seem as if mind and soul travel through dimensions inconceivable in the physical realm. As per the QOS, the conjuring up of space begins in the mind.

It is imperative to acquire essential concepts that will prove universal in any given situation one is likely to come across. The QOS is a tool that arms mankind with the knowledge of the workings of not only the world, but also of his Universe. The QOS is a conceptual lattice that applies to all things within the fabric of space as we know it, by bringing together three universal attributes that bind all entities; *unity, symmetry and polarity*.

Every so often you would hear some people use the saying 'centre yourself'. Although, it would seem that most of these people use this saying frivolously, obviously, unaware of what to centre oneself actually entails. According to the QOS, to centre oneself would require that the individual recognises the metaphysical sphere as an existent domain of energy. In addition, the QOS warrants that the individual appreciates the implications of the paradigms of the QOS (*unity, symmetry and polarity*) and the forces of the QOS (*time, light, transformation, purpose* and *uncertainty*) as being fundamental and inescapable forces of his Universe. Furthermore, the QOS insists that the individual be wary of a concept of Asian origin called Feng Shui, which deals with the arrangement and displacement of the space the individual occupies. Last but not least, to centre oneself, the QOS necessitates that the individual bears knowledge of the functionality of yet another concept of Asian origin called Qi.

In finding one's centre, breathing plays a very important role. Breathing is both a conscious and subconscious action. This is why even when one is unconscious, one's respiratory system continues to function. Inhaling and exhaling delivers oxygen and excretes carbon dioxide. Controlled breathing supplies much needed oxygen to the brain.

There is a nerve travelling from the abdomen to the brain called the Vagus nerve. This nerve is aroused by controlled breathing and a steady flow of oxygen. When the Vagus nerve is stimulated, it secretes a neurotransmitter called acetylcholine. This neurotransmitter promotes focus and composure and therefore, a clear mind. With regard to the application and the practice of the QOS, the appreciation of the benefits of controlled breathing is key.

On a small but definitive scale, the energy in and around us is both malleable and transient. It changes after every discreet, but by no means less significant, event. Between two entities, energy traverses in two ways; whether yin and yang, life and death, happiness and sadness, positive and negative, creation and destruction or male and female. One would imagine each discreet event, however significant, as a burst of accumulated energies. As highly conscious beings, these vital energies are conjured from within us. Taking into account the Asian context, these vital energies can be referred to as Qi and Feng Shui. And with regard to its application, the QOS is similar to Qi and Feng Shui. Qi and Feng Shui, just as the QOS, are at an all-encompassing degree, the ever-active and simultaneous intake/discharge of energy in space, making the perpetual conservation of energy possible.

Qi is the life force in everything and Feng Shui is the arrangement and displacement of the space one occupies. As Qi and Feng Shui, the QOS seeks to permeate everything in and around an individual and/or eneity. However, human beings are merely biological machines and therefore cannot be physically connected to all things in the Cosmos. Or can we? Well, as with Qi and Feng Shui, through the use of the QOS, one can by consolidating complementary traits between physical and ethereal energy, consciously gain access into one's extrasensory projection, making metaphysical energy possible.

For instance, if we were to find the complementary traits between the human form (physical) and the radiation of photons (ethereal), we could bridge the divide between the supposedly limited human form and the limitless ethereal realm. Fortunately, to some extent, this has become a reality. We have found ways to consolidate some of these complementary traits.

One example of these complementary traits would be that between biology and electricity. The complementary traits between biology and electricity, once harnessed and amalgamated, give us bioelectricity. Bioelectricity has a range of practical applications such as electroreception, which is the ability to detect electric fields or magnetoreception, which is the ability to detect the direction one is facing based on the Earth's magnetic field. By harnessing the energies of the physical together with the ethereal realm, mankind has discovered ways to amend the laws of physics. Having consolidated the complementary traits between the human form and the ethereal realm, we can now metaphysically connect people to their environment through a multitude of various technological means.

In theory, the QOS, when used at its optimum, should amass enough power to enable its bearer to reach all throughout the Universe. As mentioned in the foreword, symmetry between two opposite and equal forces is a simultaneous and infinite back-and-forth surge of polarization between two points, always convening at the centre. In a human being's existence, this polarization is the eternal struggle between life and death; good and bad; positive and negative, each with the need to occupy one entity. And so, unlike any other entity in the known Universe, the bearer of the QOS should have the capacity to conceive; that not only is he part of what is being perceived, but that as its sole observer, he is also its executor.

For the QOS to encapsulate its inherent forces (*time, light, transformation, purpose* and *uncertainty*) all at once, one should imagine the concept as equilibrium infinite at both ends.

It is important to note that the QOS has to be effortlessly conceivable to Man, as this is a principal feature to consider when formulating any concept. As a universal concept, it should be where all things rest. the QOS should serve as an all-encompassing synopsis of existence of the Universe and the world as we know it.

As a concept, the understanding and acquiescence of the QOS would not amount to anything if it were at all contradictory. Contradiction is one of the reasons why the bearer of the QOS needs to be rational when applying the concept, as the powerful considerations that come with its comprehension are potentially dangerous. Of all the organisms that are of Earth, Man is rational. This supremacy is accompanied by the responsibility of reasoning before acting and some would say that this is the gift and the curse of humankind in that, if one acts rationally or otherwise irrationally, he or she is beholden to the merits and demerits which come with rationale.

The QOS as an absolute concept that applies to the abstracts and concretes of the world and nature requires extensive knowledge of the world we live in; knowledge such as the comprehension of words and what they pertain to in our everyday lives. Otherwise, one would not be able to interpret this concept with complete understanding, or would they? As some of the cornerstones of conceptual acquiescence, literacy and numeracy are fundamental in a person's life. They help one gain an advanced way of creating and improving ideas of his world. This comprehension of words and numbers paves a path for the appreciation of the science and the art existence entails. Yes, the QOS requires that its bearer taps into his extrasensory projection...but, without knowledge, comprehension of the concept in itself is unrealistic.

The bearer of the QOS must prosper in solitude, otherwise its application will not be possible. This prerequisite makes provision for optimal self-introspection. Self-introspection stresses the need to be acquainted with the arrangement and displacement of the space one occupies. Once an individual is at peace with who he is, he can reflect on his thoughts with conviction. This then affords a person the opportunity to meditate on what is of most importance to him, not just in the present but also in the future.

It is pinnacle to appreciate that how one sees oneself is invaluable to understanding the mechanisms of his environment and fellow inhabitants. Retrospective introspection is one way in which an individual can go about uncovering characteristics about himself through the eyes of other people and past experiences.

It is of much importance for every single person on this planet to have the capability of understanding and applying concepts or abstracts against the backdrop of concretes of the world. The capability to retrace where and how concepts come about, is pinnacle. Humankind has the capacity to consciously grasp almost all the knowledge within the Universe in just the brain; a quality that no other entity can perform. This indicates the undisputable human ability to conceive, process and apply concepts appropriate to everything within the realm of the Universe.

The challenges most of us are faced with when applying concepts, are that of uncertainty and contradiction and this is almost every time, reflected in our morale pertaining to worldly virtues. When we do not know where we stand, we cannot measure how far we are from where we reckon we should or shouldn't be and this results in a lack of invaluable reckoning and unwavering action.

Some conceptualists have rested upon the notion that nothing is immeasurable, whether it be love, knowledge or abhorrence. As the QOS is constant as an ever-flowing process, one could never really put a finger on its full magnitude. Therefore, a person would be taking a great stride were they to, with full assurance, think they could account for its entirety. We are not omniscient and therefore, are flawed in different capacities to different degrees. Although Man is the measure of all things, he himself is immeasurably human.

Subjectivist Objectivism

It is said that, somewhere in the deserts of Egypt, contained by man-made structures in which the mummified bodies of Egyptian monarchs of the day were some time ago laid to rest, lay a mysterious supernatural force, unexplained by science. The kings and queens buried in these tombs are said to have believed these edifices to be vessels to eternal life. To their final place of rest, they took along with them their most prized worldly possessions, of which were in the form of the finest exotic fruits and precious stones. The tombs in which this illustrious energy is believed to be harnessed, the Egyptians christened The Great Pyramids of Giza.

Scientists have found evidence which suggests that the power housed in the most iconic pyramid of the three Pyramids of Giza, is a tomb belonging to a Pharaoh named Khufu. This one pyramid is known as 'The Great Pyramid of Giza'. It is said that the structure of The Great Pyramid of Giza has the ability in it to preserve organic matter, so much so that, organic matter not only grows faster, but also ripens fully and never spoils.

According to the QOS, if such a force does indeed exist within the confines of this man-made structure, then it could only be as a result of an otherwise naturally-occurring phenomenon called self-similarity. What then is self-similarity?

The Great Pyramid of Giza

Like most concepts in nature, Self-similarity is a simple yet complex one. In a few words, Self-similarity suggests that each of the definable parts of an entity, capable of being definable as being part of a collective, are similar to one another, as they may each be definable as entities of such a collective. However, each entity is not exactly identical to another, for the reason that each part is definable as singular and unique from not only the collective of entities, but also from every other singular part that makes up the collective entity. Self-similarity tells of a law of the Universe that promotes procreation, and with it individualism.

The question then becomes, what do the Great Pyramids of Giza and the enigmatic Self-similarity have to do with the QOS? Believe it or not, the answer lies in snowflakes.

The most striking of all identical characteristics or complementary traits that the great pyramid of Giza, snowflakes and self-similarity all exhibit is that they all, and in their own distinctively unique way, succumb to symmetry.

There are various kinds of symmetry and all differ in complexity, proportion and dimension. There are lines of symmetry and there are planes of symmetry. Symmetry is not just the common mirror-image, as demonstrated through bilateral symmetry. Other forms of symmetry are radial symmetry, spherical, rotational and axial symmetry.

bilateral symmetry

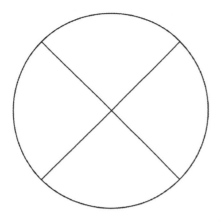

radial symmetry

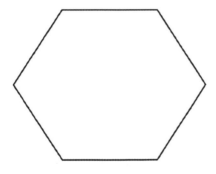

rotational symmetry

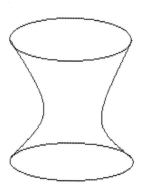

axial symmetry

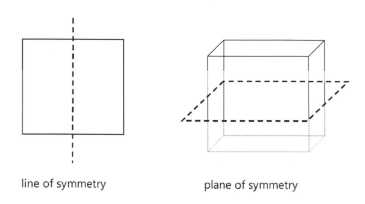

line of symmetry   plane of symmetry

The rupture of symmetry is what sees the Great pyramid of Giza, snowflakes and Self-similarity coming together to affirm the QOS as a universal concept. Just as the paradigms that bind Newton's action and reaction, symmetry would, simply by virtue of its existence, be bound by the paradigms of *unity, symmetry and polarity*. In other words, without the initial rupture of symmetry, which is thought to have taken place during the Big

Bang, the paradigms of *unity, symmetry and polarity* would not have been realised. Therefore, the Universe, or even snowflakes for that matter, would not exist.

As with any body of knowledge which seeks to hold some measure of conceptual value in order to realise a blueprint, and with it every conceivable derivative, one must create relevant and corresponding parameters. In this chapter, by using the QOS, we put this theory through its paces in an attempt to realise a blueprint that links the QOS to the seemingly unrelated Great Pyramid of Giza, snowflakes and self-similarity.

Every significant event that takes place in the Universe is subject to some form of conceptual blueprint, from the Big Bang, the conception of a child, the metamorphosis of a caterpillar, the conception of offspring, all the way to an event as seemingly mundane as the diurnal cycle of sunrise and sunset. According to the QOS, the blueprint of any such event may alter, subject to the rupture of symmetry. What this means is that only beyond a parameter bound by the paradigms of the QOS, i.e. *unity, symmetry and polarity*, in one form or another, can the blueprint of any such event change into what it may, within the constrictions of *time, light, transformation, purpose* and uncertainty; and within the confines of space. The fabric of space and time itself exists as a result of an initial rupture of symmetry, which occurred billions of years ago and is subsequently, to this day, still bound by the laws of symmetry at various levels of complexity. According to the QOS, the changes of events brought on by the rupture of symmetry are necessary, as they facilitate for the universe's most fundamental natural process of transformation. Without the rupture of symmetry, there could not have been unity nor polarity. Without the rupture of symmetry, transformation could not take place, which would therefore relate to a universe without purpose, in which nothing would happen; no positive and negative, no big bang, no snowflakes, no children, and no day and night.

Basically, what all this translates to is, life in all its simple and complex forms, is reminiscent of symmetry. Our very DNA, the building blocks of all life, is indicative of this. So, if there is any conceptual lattice that connects Man, in the present, to both his past and future, it is that of symmetry.

Of all the billions of snowflakes that have graced our planet, not once has there ever been any two snowflakes alike…well, at least not entirely. Every single snowflake to have ever existed displays symmetry in its geometric disposition. It would seem that the one characteristic about snowflakes that provides for their uniqueness also happens to be the very same characteristic that makes them similar to one another. This phenomenon is called self-similarity. Adorned with an infinite number of intricate designs, snowflakes are a demonstration of Mother Nature's need to uphold fundamental order and always with a touch of insatiable beauty. In her snowflakes, she reveals to us that being different from the rest is, in fact, one of the many similar characteristics or complementary traits which we all as entities possess. Furthermore, she shows us the sheer power of a single entity, be it a sub-atomic particle or a whole planet, against all other entities that inhabit the length and breadth of space.

One could assume that just as the unique yet symmetry-bound snowflake, the dimensions of one of The Great Pyramid of Giza exhibits that of self-similarity. It could be said that the self-similarity in The Great Pyramid of Giza is epitomised at the pyramid's summit on account of its geometric dimensions. However, were one to reduce the geometric dimensions of the Great Pyramid of Giza as a whole to a scale of 1:3, which is one third of the pyramid, the dimensions of the 1:3 would mean that the one third of the initial pyramid still would be in itself a pyramid. This simply means that the Great Pyramid of Giza is made up of more than one pyramid.

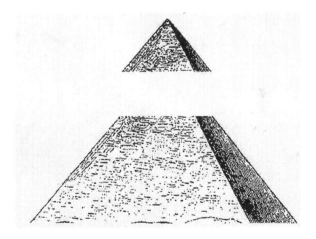

Pyramid scale of 1:3

As mentioned before, to realise a pattern, one must create relevant and corresponding parameters. So, the summit or the top third of the pyramid, where the power of The Great Pyramid of Giza is concentrated is, because of the pyramid's geometric dimensions, the most crucial proportion of The Great Pyramid of Giza's symmetry. This therefore begs the need to establish how nature rations the distribution of *unity, symmetry and polarity*, which brings us to what is called Fibonacci's Golden Mean.

Fibonacci's Golden Mean, otherwise known as Phi, is a geometric consequence that appears in physics, astronomy, botany, zoology, human anatomy, DNA, the solar system, music, snowflakes and The Great Pyramid of Giza.

Phi is the ratio 1:1,618. For instance, the spiralled shape of a seashell is evidence of the genesis of its formation. This is seen by how many revolutions from the centre of the sea shell's spiral have coiled outwards toward its extremes. Every revolution from inside-out is bigger than the next in width, with the difference between each complete revolution being the ratio 1:1,618.

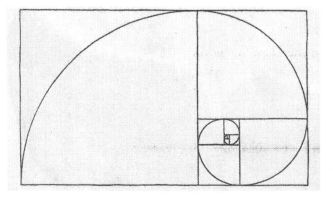

Fibonacci's Golden Mean

The average person's middle finger is 0,618 times smaller than his hand, as is his hand when compared to his forearm and his forearm to his whole arm.

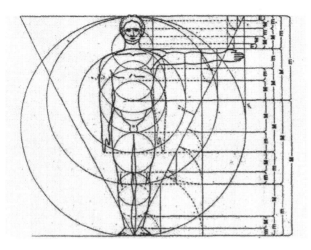

The Ratio 1:0,618

Therefore, the most insatiable question becomes, could Fibonacci's Golden Mean be the answer to how the Universe rations the distribution of *unity, symmetry and polarity*?

Vim and Vigour

The feeling of nostalgia we are overcome by when gazing at the stars is no coincidence. Just as the lapping of water, the flares of fire, the feeling of a breeze of fresh air or the scent of wet earth, the stars evoke something in us. One remarkable attribute, which each of these elements share, is the authority to spawn both calm and turbulence, all at Mother Nature's will. Throughout the Cosmos, in all of space and matter, there reverberates a unified force of energy. It is an energy so influential yet so discreet; so powerful and yet so modest. Graced by her living examples, it becomes clear that Mother Nature is a benevolent dictator, but nevertheless, a dictator. "God has subjected all of the Cosmos to Man", with human beings possessing an unsurpassed ability to interact, not only between themselves, but also with their Universe. But, there seems to be more to it than that.

It is only natural to be admirers of Mankind and all the nature with which he has been blessed. How we mindfully perceive the world is the currency between Mother Nature and ourselves. The interdependence between humans and nature is misunderstood by some, and even worse, neglected by most. In this day in age, our concern about nature tends to become conspicuous more by its absence than otherwise. As much as we claim to be part of it, little evidence of that can be seen and this is the folly of Man.

The world, depending on how one looks at it, is either a paradise or a hellish place. One thing for sure, it is not meant for the faint-hearted. By looking at the way things are in the world, it has become ever more apparent that, we the people of the world, lack love for Mankind and Nature. We are, at an accelerated rate of transgression, descending into a void of a meaningless existence. It is as if we are in search of something that we know is there but are not sure what its actual value is. We are in a paradoxical predicament. We have to decide between two crucial choices. One choice being that we as the people of the world, pro-actively give back to Nature and Mankind and contrarily, is for us to continuously take from Nature and Mankind. This decision, once made, will determine what kind of world we want to become. Although, it is important to express that the betterment or detriment of Nature and Mankind hangs not in the hands of the world, but in that of the individual's.

For posterity, there is no individual more instrumental than the youth. The youth is the world's bridge between the old and the new ways of doing things. However, this inherent power to change the future of the world does not come without its challenges. From a tender age, youth are introduced into rigid learning systems, as if they were all the same. As a result, most become divergent, as a cause of being siphoned with sometimes unnecessary and redundant content on an everyday basis for years on end. Because of a lack of understanding, institutions and society can sometimes think of these divergent thinkers to be failures and rebels.

A youth's mind is as delicate as glass and goes where the wind blows. If a youth's potential in a learning area, be it physical or mental, has been recognized, it would only seem right that somebody steer the youth in the right direction, without arbitrarily removing the youth's liberty of choice based just on a predetermined educational system. The youth is, by virtue of being a scholar, coerced to consign to a career that would best suit its individual interests, but in most cases, the youth ends up stranded at a place where it thought it knew really well, in search of refuge in adolescence. This almost every time transcends to juvenile delinquency. The possibilities are endless if a youth's talents have been harnessed and honed. Each youth is like a filament and given enough attention, he or she could brighten up the world. A youth's mind will constantly conceive rash but powerful ideas. These ideas will ultimately shape the youth as he or she crosses the threshold through puberty into adulthood and beyond.

Each youth deserves to be given the privilege of a quality elementary education. This way, the youth can learn simple and complex concepts, dependent on his or her mental and/or physical initiative. This, in turn, will develop capacity to reason accordingly and ultimately, the youth will become a fully-fledged, reassured individual.

Through the internet and various social networks, the youth are more interactive. They are more exposed and are more forgiving to the diverse and sometimes contradictive traits of the world. The youth has a more reassured sense of who they are, both as individuals and as a collective. There are infinite areas at which the youth can excel in terms of academic and creative platforms, be they traditional or unorthodox. One's achievement is weighed by how successful he or she is, in whatever it is they do. And the youth are taught to resemble 'larger than life' figures in their respective fields. Still, whether or not the older generation realises it, the youth are making their own strides in a world which they have inherited from their predecessors. This transition may seem ordinary, but it is not so. And one can tell this just by taking a look at the rate at which the world is advancing.

It would seem that when most people reflect on the future of the world, the first thing that comes to mind is the chaos and the imminent demise of Earth and all life on it. As luck would have it, there is not one person to blame for what the world has since become and if there were, perhaps we all would have to be held liable. Nevertheless, these critical thoughts are appropriate. However, instead of hopelessly pointing fingers at each other in search of scapegoats, we ought to unite, for the sake of our children and their children not to bear the consequences of the mistakes we and our forefathers have made.

As the impending rupture of 'Nature versus The World' has befallen us, it is time for change. We should be alarmed, because even with all the technology in the world, humans could never duplicate another planet like the Earth. Whether or not we had decreased high-in-carbon chemicals and preserved the Earth as best as we could, in the long run, the Earth would have still later than never, killed everything in it to renew itself. Today we are no longer just fighting amongst ourselves, but the Earth is fighting against the world. It is prudent to say that it's a fight that we will indefinitely lose, but how we lose it is entirely up to us.

We are a dynamic species with a tempestuous past and an uncertain future. Our time here on Earth has seen Man create and destroy. In the pursuit of peace and order, we have developed various forms of faiths and laws, coupled with their own set of principles. These faiths and laws in turn, have guided Mankind to a somewhat agreeable state of civilisation. But even these faiths and laws that Man aligns himself with, have evident grave downsides as history will tell, of a matter which begs the need to take a closer look at not only the culture of the world, but also at the mind of the individual.

Anything born of Nature is a forecast of a perpetual continuum. Something good can easily transcend to something bad and vice versa. This change does not put forward the unquestionable fact that whatever thing born out of nature be no longer a single entity. In other words, the easiest way to tell one thing from another is the absence of resemblance.

At one time or another, you have looked outside yourself and in that moment, felt as if you had a little piece of paradise in the palm of your hand, seemingly in control of your space. Soon after, another feeling hits you.

Then suddenly, you are slowly but inevitably headed back towards imminent reality, as you just can't distance yourself from it for too long. This internal conflict driven by thoughts of being inadequate and adequate drives you to begin to question an idea you yourself, planted in your own head. Thereafter, notions of your flawed, apparent world arise. And finally, you comfort yourself in the acceptance of how human you really are. This perpetual continuum of thought could happen within a matter of seconds.

The above just goes to show how even the most discreet of things, such as thought, experience an array of conflict and reconciliation. Yes, we each would love for everything to go as anticipated, sometimes unforgiving to the grand scheme of things. As change has proven time and time again, in pursuit for the greater good, conflict is sometimes necessary. Yet, good will always be the best means to an end.

Of course, there are times when we erroneously yearn for authority over the world's unpredictability. And there are times when we wholly appreciate the bliss we enjoy, as if, were we to have insatiable insight into the workings of the Universe, we would be overwhelmed and would surely beyond the shadow of a doubt be engulfed by its awe-inspiring profundity. Certainly, for the average human being, this demanding grandeur of existence would not be a life enjoyed. Although, it should be said that we should all see it fit that the lifelong expedition of the exploration of the metaphysical sphere be delegated to

Man, as we have an ability second to none that enables us to connect with our Universe.

As Mankind, we all exhibit similarities in our individual uniqueness. We enjoy a higher level of consciousness in comparison to every other living organism on earth. Humans have a more advanced knowledge-base and possess the ability to employ nature. We are blessed with the mental faculty to be metaphysically attuned to the Universe. Man has been granted the ability to perceive seemingly everything. But the reality is that, all the knowledge in the world is an insatiable indulgence that could never be gulped down by any one being. This is why it is vital to acknowledge that in order to have purpose in this world, one has to find and occupy his or her own designated space, as each and every one of us has one.

Space begins in the mind

Printed in the United States
By Bookmasters